Summer SPLASH TRAVEL ACTIVITY BOOK

Brighter Child®
An imprint of Carson-Dellosa Publishing LLC
Greensboro, North Carolina

Brighter Child®
An imprint of Carson-Dellosa Publishing LLC
P.O. Box 35665
Greensboro, NC 27425 USA

ISBN 978-1-62399-110-4

01-060131151

Table of Contents

Table of Contents

TRAVEL GAMES TIPS

Travel games are a great way to break up the boredom of a long distance trip. Guessing games, word games, and memory games provide hours of fun and learning. Use this section to help you plan ahead to get even more fun out of your travels!

Portable Fun Pak

Before your trip, gather together a "fun pak"—a set of things that will help you occupy your time while traveling. Choose items that are small and portable. Place them in a backpack or a tote bag.

Skim through the ideas in this book and mark the games you think you'd like to play on your trip. Some games require you to prepare something before your trip. Be sure to include any materials needed for those activities in your fun pak. Refer to the **What to Take** list on page 7 for some suggestions.

What and how much you take will depend on how long you plan to travel. Also, some things that are appropriate for one form of travel may not be ideal for another.

What To Take

Here are some suggestions for your fun pak. Remember not to take too much. You don't want your fun pak to be more burden than fun.

Items needed to use with this book:

- ✔ crayons
- ✔ a deck of playing cards
- ✔ a large pad of paper
- ✔ paper lunch bags

- ✔ pencils/pens/ markers
- ✔ steno pad or lined journal
- ✔ watch with a second hand

List other things you want to take on your trip here:

_____

_____   _____

_____   _____

_____   _____

NUMBER GAMES

At the end of their preschool year, children should be fluent in counting from **0** to **20**. There are plenty of ways for your child to practice counting while on the go—you just need to know where to look!

Important Numbers

Make a list of numbers that are important to you in some way. Then, as you travel, look for those numbers on road signs, license plates, billboards, and buildings. Check off the numbers on your list as you see them.

SOME IMPORTANT NUMBERS:

- your age
- the ages of the people in your family
- the day of your birthday (such as 27 or 427 if you were born on April 27)
- today's date
- the first three digits of your phone number
- your street number
- the number of people in your family

MY IMPORTANT NUMBERS

_____   _____
_____   _____
_____   _____
_____   _____
_____   _____

Pick A Number

You'll need a deck of cards for this game. First, take out the joker, ace, king, queen, and jack. Then, place the remaining cards in a lunch bag.

Each player takes a turn picking a card from the bag. The one who selects the highest card keeps the cards of the other players. If more than one card shows the same number, those players draw another card. The player with the highest card keeps all the cards.

Continue until all the cards from the bag have been selected or there are not enough cards for another round. The players count their cards. The winner is the one with the greatest number of cards.

Number Lotto

Use the lotto gameboards below and on pages 12–14. Have each player write a number from **0** to **20** in the 16 sections. Next, have everyone try to spot the numbers that are on his or her gameboard. The first person to spot a number calls it out and crosses it off his or her gameboard. Players who have that same number do not cross it off their gameboards; only the first person to spot the number gets to cross it off. The player who crosses off the most numbers is the winner.

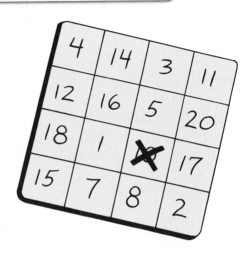

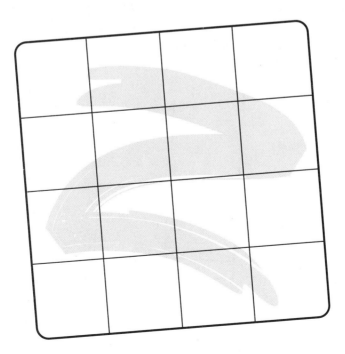

Number Lotto

(Directions are found on page 11.)

Number Lotto

(Directions are found on page 11.)

Number Lotto

(Directions are found on page 11.)

FABULOUS WORD SEARCH PUZZLES

Word search puzzles encourage children to use problem solving and creative thinking skills to recognize words hidden in the puzzle. It also provides excellent practice in recognizing common sight words.

I Can Read It!

Find and circle the words in the puzzle.

a	n	d	b	u	p
s	e	e	k	a	t
c	i	s	p	w	r
f	o	d	n	o	t
e	r	u	n	h	f
j	i	n	t	h	e
i	t	m	v	g	o

and   to   at   go

in   its   it   not

run   see   the   up

Find and circle the words in the puzzle.

```
x  a  c  o  r  n  e  w
c  s  a  x  i  k  w  a
x  a  c  a  d  d  o  p
n  n  e  m  a  d  t  e
z  t  f  v  c  g  a  h
z  o  f  a  p  p  l  e
```

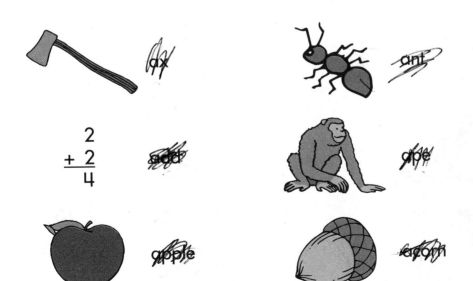

ax

ant

$\begin{array}{r} 2 \\ + 2 \\ \hline 4 \end{array}$

add

ape

apple

acorn

Super S

Find and circle the words in the puzzle.

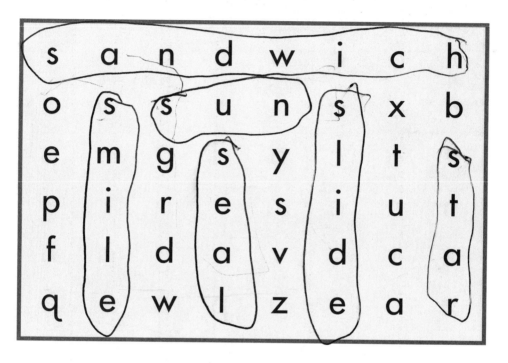

s	a	n	d	w	i	c	h
o	s	s	u	n	s	x	b
e	m	g	s	y	l	t	s
p	i	r	e	s	i	u	t
f	l	d	a	v	d	c	a
q	e	w	l	z	e	a	r

sun

star

seal

slide

sandwich

Living Things

Find and circle the words in the puzzle.

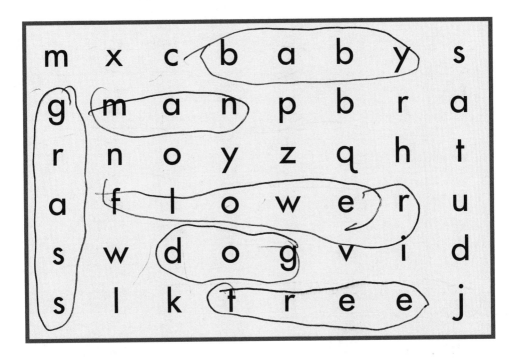

```
m  x  c  b  a  b  y  s
g  m  a  n  p  b  r  a
r  n  o  y  z  q  h  t
a  f  l  o  w  e  r  u
s  w  d  o  g  v  i  d
s  l  k  t  r  e  e  j
```

dog

man

tree

baby

grass

flower

In the Ocean

Find and circle the words in the puzzle.

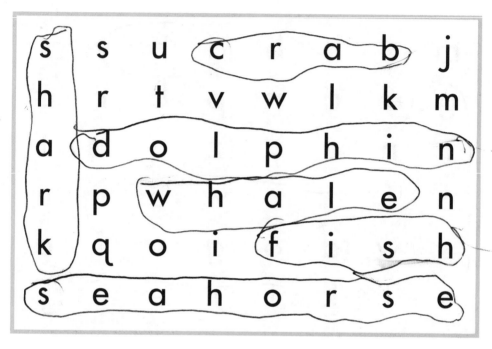

s s u c r a b j
h r t v w l k m
a d o l p h i n
r p w h a l e n
k q o i f i s h
s e a h o r s e

fish

crab

whale

shark

dolphin

seahorse

Toy Time

Find and circle the words in the puzzle.

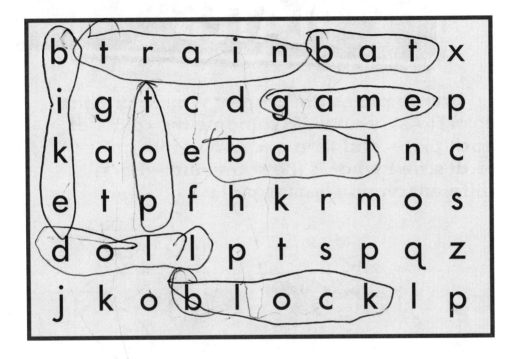

b	t	r	a	i	n	b	a	t	x
i	g	t	c	d	g	a	m	e	p
k	a	o	e	b	a	l	l	n	c
e	t	p	f	h	k	r	m	o	s
d	o	l	l	p	t	s	p	q	z
j	k	o	b	l	o	c	k	l	p

train
ball
doll
bike
block
ball
top
game

FUN WITH LICENSE PLATES

License plates are a great way to practice colors! Ask your child to name the colors of each plate, and then encourage him or her to describe what is the same and what is different among license plates.

Out-of-State Plates

Be on the lookout for out-of-state license plates. When you find one, call out the state where the license plate was issued. Score 1 point for every out-of-state plate you spot first. The first person who scores 20 points wins.

License Plate Collection

Try to spot as many different kinds of license plates as you can. Here are some things you can look for: place name, color, slogan, picture, or symbol. List the kinds of license plates you see. Use the recording sheet on pages 25 and 26.

FLORIDA XGY 84K

875·AB WISCONSIN

LME·95 COLORADO

Variation: Collect license plates by state or province. List the ones you see. At the end of your trip, tally how many you've collected.

License Plate Collection

(Directions are found on page 24.)

MY LIST

_____

_____

_____

_____

_____

_____

_____

_____

_____

_____

MY LIST

_____

_____

_____

_____

_____

_____

_____

_____

_____

_____

License Plate Collection

(Directions are found on page 24.)

MY LIST

_____

_____

_____

_____

_____

_____

_____

_____

_____

_____

_____

MY LIST

_____

_____

_____

_____

_____

_____

_____

_____

_____

_____

_____

License Plate Lotto

Use the lotto gameboards below and on pages 28–30. Each player fills in the 25 sections with numbers from **1** to **9** and letters of the alphabet. The numbers and letters may be used more than once.

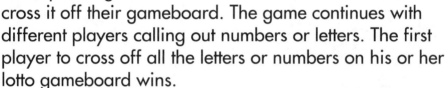

Next, one player calls out a number or a letter from the license plate of a passing vehicle. Players with the corresponding number or letter will cross it off their gameboard. The game continues with different players calling out numbers or letters. The first player to cross off all the letters or numbers on his or her lotto gameboard wins.

License Plate Lotto

(Directions are found on page 27.)

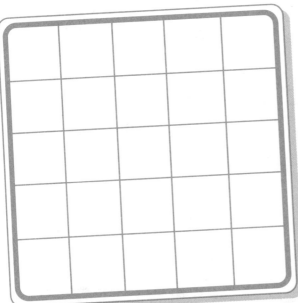

License Plate Lotto

(Directions are found on page 27.)

License Plate Lotto

(Directions are found on page 27.)

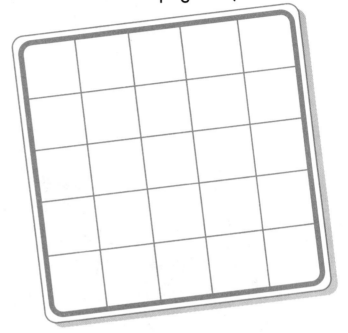

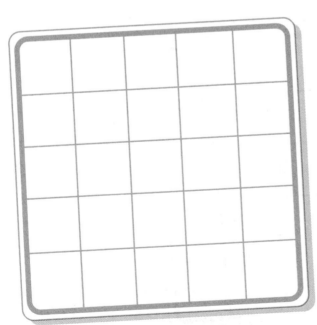

CAN YOU SPOT THAT?

Observation is the first step in forming critical thinking skills. Observation skills allow your child to notice and understand what's going on around him or her, which gives your child practice in early skills of compare and contrast and similarities and differences.

Food Fun

Use the Food Fun lists below and on pages 33 and 34. See how many food words or pictures of food you can find while traveling. Look for them on billboards, restaurant signs, and other sources. See how many items you can spot in 30 minutes.

FOOD FUN LIST

_____

_____

_____

_____

_____

_____

_____

FOOD FUN LIST

_____

_____

_____

_____

_____

_____

_____

Food Fun

(Directions are found on page 32.)

FOOD FUN LIST

_____

_____

_____

_____

_____

_____

_____

_____

_____

_____

FOOD FUN LIST

_____

_____

_____

_____

_____

_____

_____

_____

_____

_____

Food Fun

(Directions are found on page 32.)

FOOD FUN LIST

_____

_____

_____

_____

_____

_____

_____

_____

_____

_____

FOOD FUN LIST

_____

_____

_____

_____

_____

_____

_____

_____

_____

_____

Traveler's Tic Tac Toe

This game requires two players sitting next to each other. One person is **X** and the other is **O**.

Use the grids below and on pages 36–38. Write in each section the name of something you might see during your travels, such as a stop sign or a fire hydrant. The first player to see one of the items calls it out and writes his or her designated letter in the corresponding place on the grid. The first person to get three in a row wins.

Traveler's Tic Tac Toe

(Directions are found on page 35.)

Traveler's Tic Tac Toe

(Directions are found on page 35.)

Traveler's Tic Tac Toe

(Directions are found on page 35.)

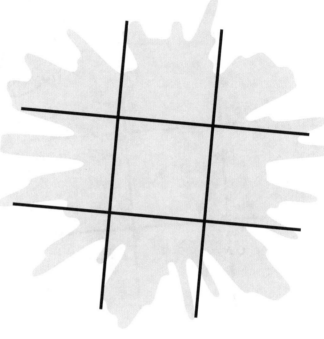

Traveler's Scavenger Hunt

Here's a fun scavenger hunt that everyone in the car will enjoy playing.

Together, make a list of 12 or more things you will most likely see on your trip. The list can include general things, such as a billboard or a farm, and very specific items, such as a black-and-white cow or a sign that displays the letter **Z**.

While traveling, everyone helps look for the things on the list. The first person to spot an item calls it out, then writes his or her initial beside that item on the list. If two people call out an item at the same time, both their initials are written down. The goal is to find as many things on the list as possible within a given amount of time or before the trip is over. (Lists are found on pages 40–42.)

Traveler's Scavenger Hunt

(Directions are found on page 39.)

MY LIST

1. _____
2. _____
3. _____
4. _____
5. _____
6. _____
7. _____
8. _____
9. _____
10. _____
11. _____
12. _____

MY LIST

1. _____
2. _____
3. _____
4. _____
5. _____
6. _____
7. _____
8. _____
9. _____
10. _____
11. _____
12. _____

Traveler's Scavenger Hunt

(Directions are found on page 39.)

MY LIST		MY LIST	
1.		1.	raddit
2.		2.	timosen
3.		3.	list
4.		4.	person
5.		5.	statue
6.		6.	dog
7.		7.	leash
8.		8.	leaf
9.		9.	rake
10.		10.	sidewalk
11.		11.	snack
12.		12.	mud

Traveler's Scavenger Hunt

(Directions are found on page 39.)

MY LIST

1. Sgin
2. house
3. car
4. van
5. yards
6. garbge
7. toys
8. seat
9. 6 tires
10. truck
11. sky
12. sun

MY LIST

1. racoon
2. tent
3. Flag pole
4. Hydrant
5. red roof
6. Blue door
7. door
8. crat
9. Bear
10. moster
11. tree
12. motel

Roadside Bingo

Use the bingo cards below and on pages 44–47. Players fill in the sections with various things they might see on their trip, such as a black cat, a flagpole, a white van, and a fire hydrant. When players see one of the items on their bingo card, they cross it off. The first person to make a straight line vertically, horizontally, or diagonally calls out "Bingo!" and wins.

Roadside Bingo

(Directions are found on page 43.)

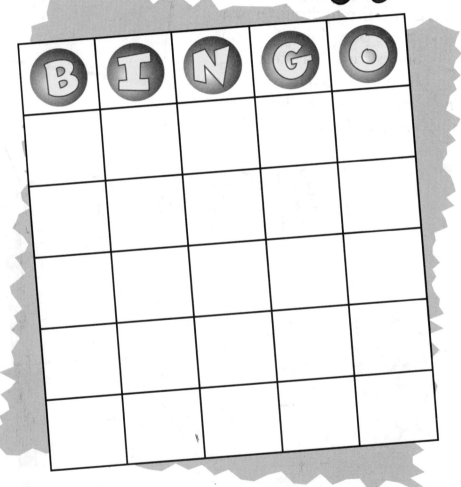

Roadside Bingo

(Directions are found on page 43.)

Roadside Bingo

(Directions are found on page 43.)

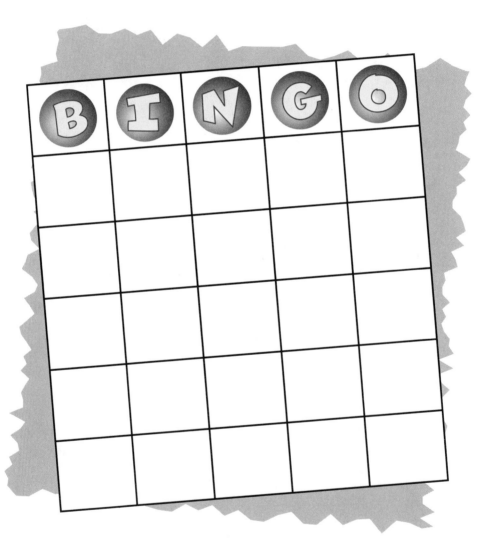

Roadside Bingo

(Directions are found on page 43.)

Spot the Signs

See how many of the following signs you can spot while you're traveling. (The meaning of each sign is shown by its picture.) Check off each sign that you find.

School Crossing

Hill

No Left Turn

Deer Crossing

Food

Gas

Curve Ahead

No U Turn

Pedestrian Crosswalk

Slippery When Wet

What a Pace

Number the pictures **1, 2, 3, 4** to show the order from fastest to slowest.

2   4   3   1

3   4   1   2

4   1   3   2

MEMORY GAMES

Listening skills are very important for children of all ages. Memory games can help your child become a good listener by challenging him or her to pay attention, comprehend what he or she has heard, and then tell it back to you.

Packing a Suitcase

In this traditional game, a player starts off by saying, "I'm packing a suitcase and I'm putting in a. . . ." The player then completes the sentence with an object. The second player repeats the sentence plus adds another item. The game continues with a new item being added each time. A player who forgets an item or says it out of order is out of the game. The winner is the last person left who can state all the items that are in the suitcase.

Guess Who I Saw?

This game is similar to "Packing a Suitcase" except that you have to remember people's names. The first player begins by saying, "I went to the store and guess who I saw! My friend _____!" The player completes the sentence with a person's name. The second player then repeats what the first player said but adds another person's name: "I went to the store and guess who I saw! My friends _____ and _____!" The game continues with a different person's name being added each time. The winner is the person who can say all the names.

MUSICAL FUN

Even music can be used as a teaching tool! Here is one idea: Sing "This Old Man" with your child. Ask him or her to use fingers to represent the numbers. This allows your child to visualize the number as he or she is verbalizing it, which will help strengthen your child's understanding of number concepts.

Car-Tunes

See how quickly you can recognize tunes with this musical challenge. Turn on your radio or shuffle a playlist. Listen for a few seconds and turn off the music. Can you name that tune? If not, turn on the music and listen again. The first person to identify the song scores 1 point. Keep playing until someone scores 10 points.

Variation: Instead of naming the title of the song, players have to identify the recording artist.

Hum a Melody

One player begins by humming a tune. The tune may be from a popular song or from a melody used in a commercial, TV show, or movie. The player who identifies the tune gets to hum the next one.

CATEGORY GAMES

Category games are great for on-the-go fun and learning. All you need is paper, pencil, and your brain! Children will stretch their minds to think of objects to fit into each category. It is also a fun way for your preschooler to practice basic skills of sorting and classifying.

Color My World

One person states a color and everyone takes turns naming one thing that is that color. Keep playing until you can't think of anything else to name. Then, another person chooses a different color.

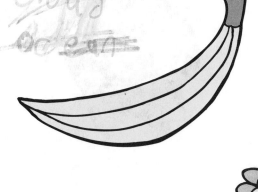

Variation: Make the game more challenging by allowing only things that naturally come in a particular color. For example, if the color were yellow, you could say "banana" or "daffodil" but not "car."

Movie Trivia

Do you like movies? Then, this category game is just for you!

One person begins by naming a movie. Then, each player takes a turn naming a character or an actor from the movie. Everyone helps to collect as many names as possible.

Variation: Play this game with two teams, and have each team write down the names on a sheet of paper. The team with the longest list wins.

TAKE A GUESS

Like category games, guessing games encourage your child to think outside the box. He or she will stretch his or her critical thinking skills in order to find the correct answer. These games are great for on-the-go learning because all you need is you and your brain!

Twenty Questions

One player starts the game by thinking of a person, place, or thing. Then, the other players take turns asking questions that can be answered by "yes" or "no." (Examples: Are you thinking of a person? Is the person a movie star?) You can keep asking questions until someone makes a correct guess or until you've reached 20 questions.

Players who think they have the answer can make a guess when it's their turn. A player who makes an incorrect guess is out. The player who guesses correctly gets to think of the next person, place, or thing.

ESP

You'll need a deck of cards to play "ESP" (Extra-Sensory Perception). Hold the cards facedown. Then, sort the cards into two piles. Place the ones you think are black in one pile and the ones you think are red in the other. Turn over the piles and count how many cards you sorted correctly. What was your ESP score?

Try this game with one or more other players. See who can get the highest ESP score.

CLEVER COLORING

These hands-on coloring activities provide your child with a visual tool, allowing him or her to clearly see and comprehend different colors and their names. Coloring to reveal the hidden pictures will also spark your child's creativity and innovation.

A Sign of Fall

Color the space yellow if the word names a color.

Color the space green if the word names a number.

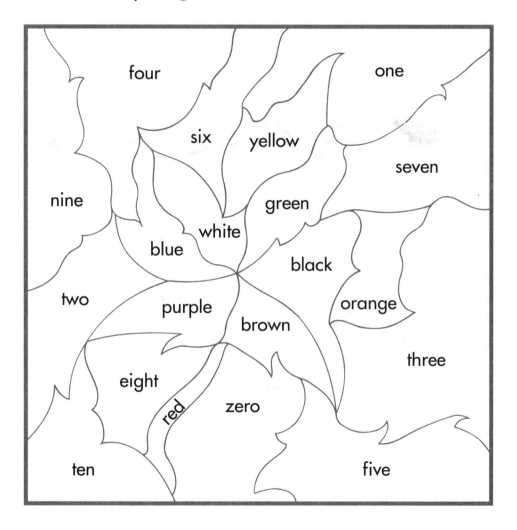

A Big Eater

Color the spaces with **B purple**.

Color the spaces with **b green**.

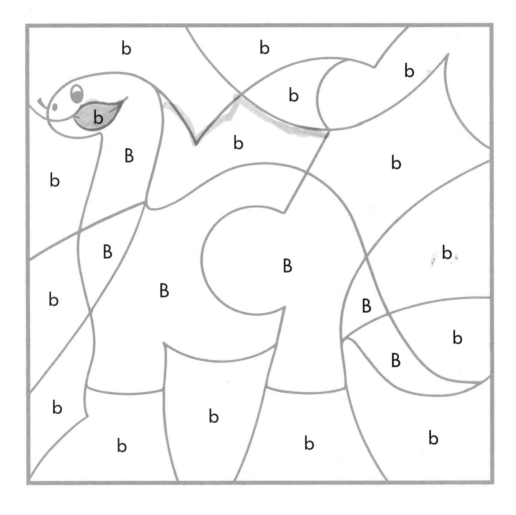

What Waves in the Wind?

Color to find the hidden picture.

★ ★ ★ = purple

★ ★
★ ★ = blue

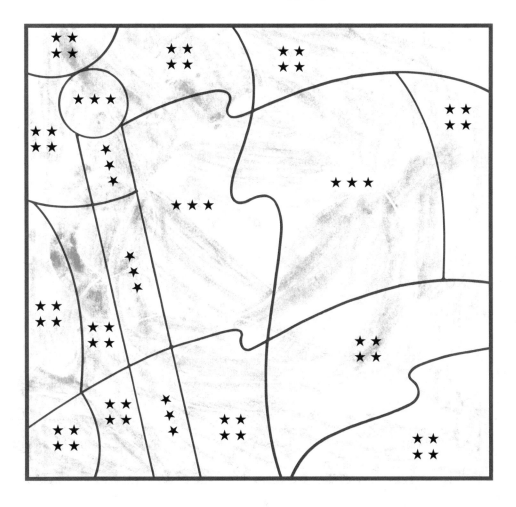

Tea Time

Color the spaces with **K blue**.

Color the spaces with **L purple**.

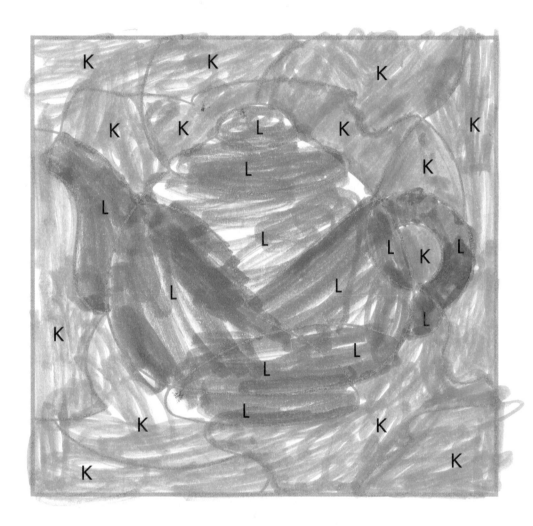

Gobble, Gobble!

Color to find the hidden picture.

6 = red   **7 = brown**   8 = yellow

9 = green   **10 = blue**

Ready for Rain

Color the spaces with **s red**.

Color the spaces with **t blue**.

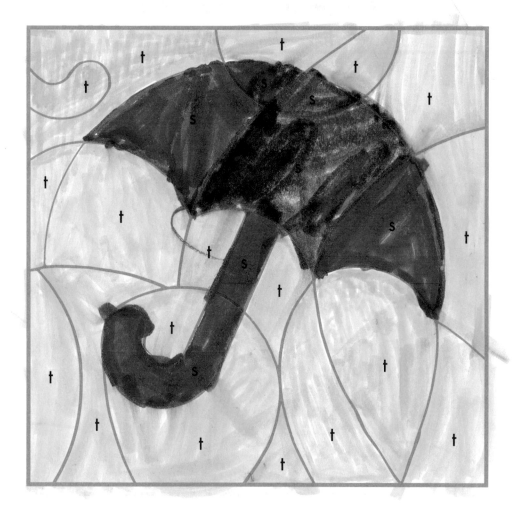

WORD CHALLENGE GAMES

Whether it's making up a silly language or playing a game in which a certain word can not be said aloud, your child will be forced to think on his or her feet, therefore improving concentration. Just watch your child's imagination expand!

Pig Latin, Please

Have you ever spoken pig Latin? The rules are easy! Just take English words and do the following:

 Move a consonant or a consonant blend from the front of a word to the end of it and add "ay." For example, "car" becomes "ar-cay" and "speak" becomes "eak-spay."

 Leave a word that begins with a vowel as is except add "ay" to the end. For example, "open" becomes "open-ay."

Try speaking pig Latin with your family during part of your trip. *aybe-May ou'll-yay ind-fay it's-ay un-fay!*

Everyone agrees not to say a certain word during a set time period. The word should be a common word such as "yes," "no," "time," or "it." Then, whenever a person says the forbidden word, he or she gets 1 point. The person with the least number of points at the end of the time period is the winner.

Silly Language

Make up your own silly language and use it for however long you like while you're traveling. Here are some ideas you can try.

Add a syllable to the end of every word. For example, *This-ee game-ee is-ee fun-ee* means *This game is fun.*

Move the last word in the sentence to the front. For example, *Snack I'd like a* means *I'd like a snack.*

Replace real words with silly words. For example, you can use *gork* for *radio*, *meeble* for *car*, and so on.

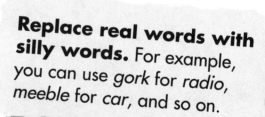

Make every other word a color word. For example, *Look red at yellow that blue cat* means *Look at that cat.*

DOT-TO-DOTS AND MAZES

Dot-to-dots are great tools for helping your preschool student practice his or her alphabet and numbers. Mazes also encourage your child's thinking skills, as he or she must think ahead to make it through to the end.

What Is Hatching?

Connect the dots from **1** to **10**.

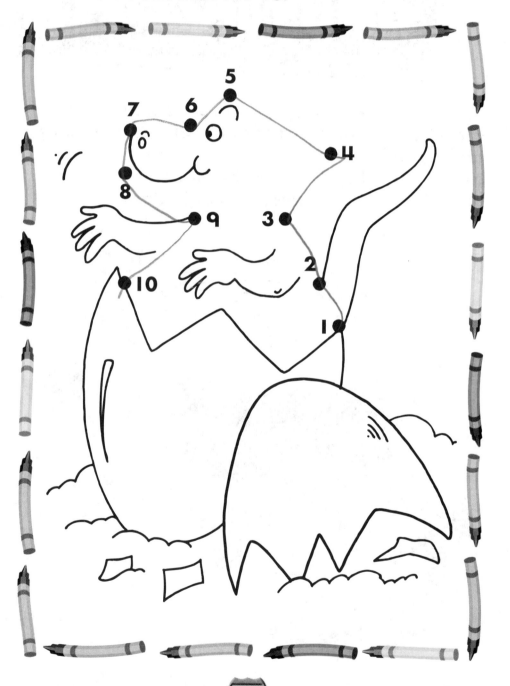

Connect the dots from **1** to **10**.

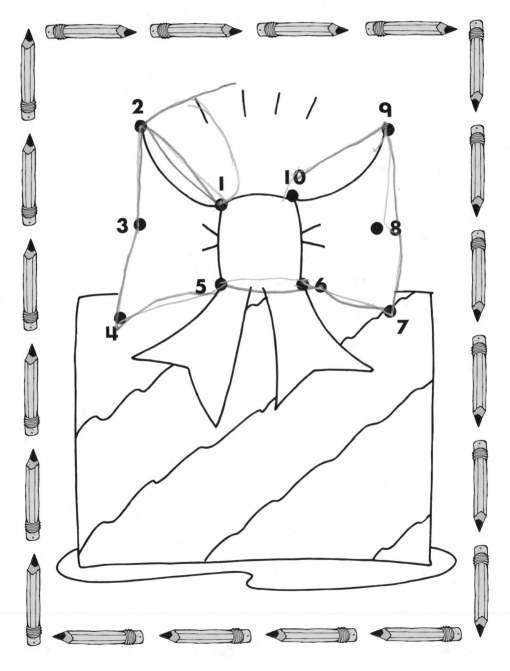

What Is Hiding in the Desert?

Connect the dots from **A** to **N**.

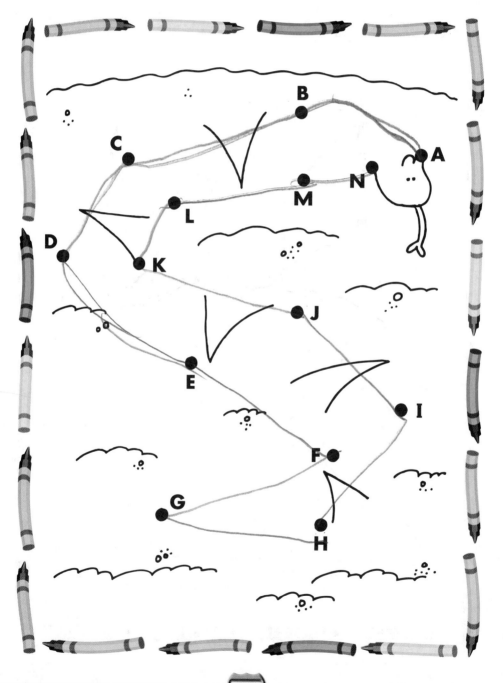

What Is on the Breakfast Table?

Connect the dots from **1** to **20**.

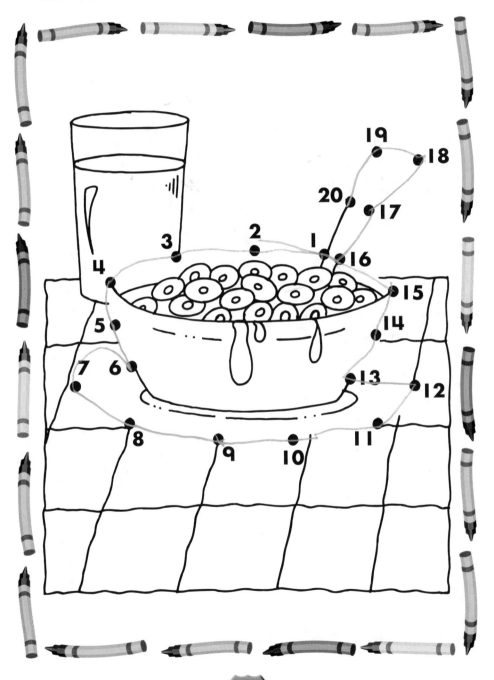

What Is Hiding in the Meadow?

Connect the dots from **A** to **W**.

Which Way to the Lodge?

Help the lost skier find her way to the ski lodge.

Which Way to the Dock?

Help the sailboat find its way to the dock.

Which Way to School?

Help the girl find the schoolhouse.

WHAT AN IMAGINATION!

These imagination games are helping your child learn to solve problems, and even develop vocabulary. Encouraging your child to be creative with these imagination activities is a great way to practice these skills and have fun while on the go!

Squiggle Art

Can you make a work of art out of a squiggle line? If you use your imagination, you can!

Play this game with another person. Use the spaces below and on pages 84 and 85. Both of you will draw a squiggle line on your paper. Then, trade papers and make an interesting picture using the squiggle as part of the drawing. You're sure to be impressed by the results!

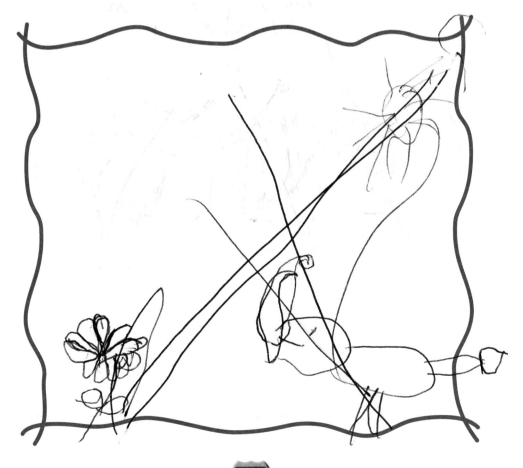

Squiggle Art

(Directions found on page 83.)

Squiggle Art

(Directions found on page 83.)

Don't Laugh

Each player tries to make the others laugh by making funny faces, telling a joke, singing in a crazy way, and so on. Tickling is not allowed, though! A person who laughs is out of the game. The last one left is, of course, the winner! Then, draw some of the funny faces you made on pages 87 and 88.

Draw Funny Faces

Draw Funny Faces

Boxed In

Use the gameboards on this page and on pages 90 and 91.

Two people can play this strategy game. Each player takes a turn drawing a line to connect a pair of dots either horizontally or vertically. When a line is drawn so that a box is made, that player

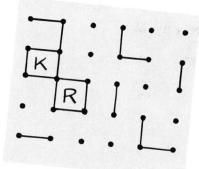

writes the first letter of his or her name inside the box and claims it. After all the dots have been connected, the players count how many boxes each has made. The one with the most boxes wins.

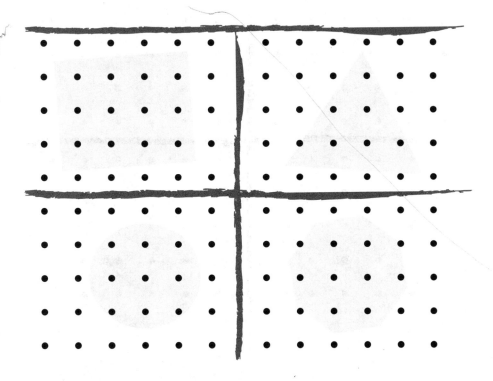

Boxed In

(Directions are found on page 89.)

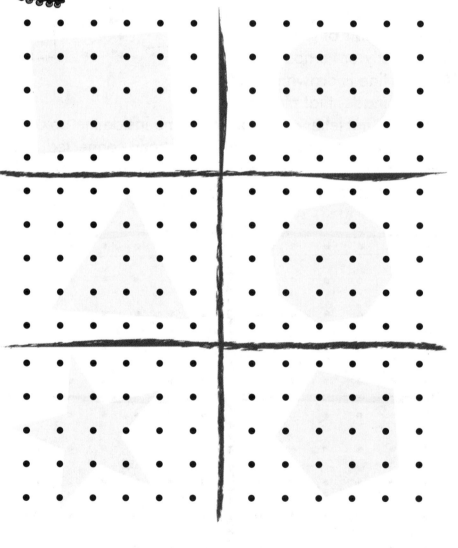

Boxed In

(Directions are found on page 89.)

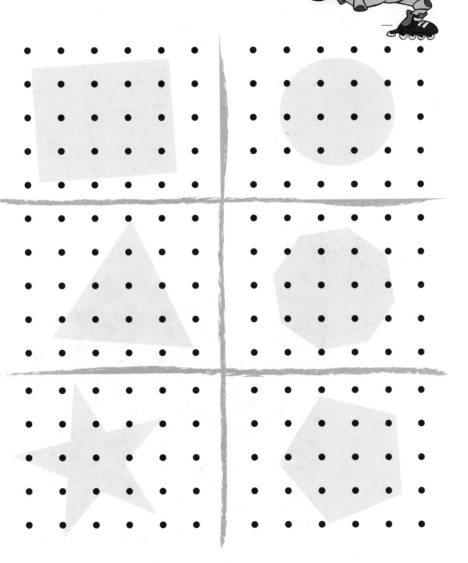

ANSWER KEY

Answer Key

I Can Read It!
Find and circle the words in the puzzle.

and	to	at	go
in	is	it	not
run	see	the	up

16

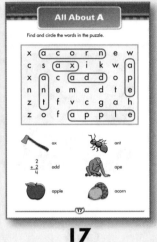

All About A
Find and circle the words in the puzzle.

ax
add
apple

ant
ape
acorn

17

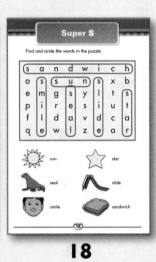

Super S
Find and circle the words in the puzzle.

sun
seal
smile

star
slide
sandwich

18

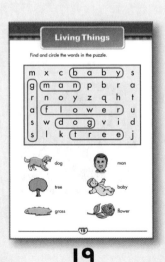

Living Things
Find and circle the words in the puzzle.

dog
tree
grass

man
baby
flower

19

In the Ocean
Find and circle the words in the puzzle.

fish
whale
dolphin

crab
shark
seahorse

20

Toy Time
Find and circle the words in the puzzle.

train
bat
block

doll
bike
ball

top
game

21

Answer Key

49

63

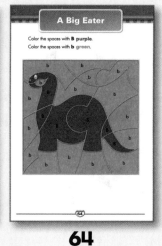

64

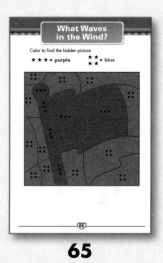

65

66

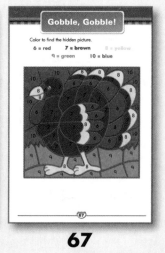

67

Answer Key

68

74

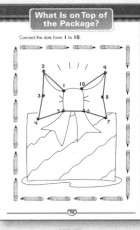

75

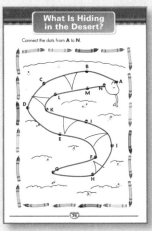

76

77

78

Answer Key

79

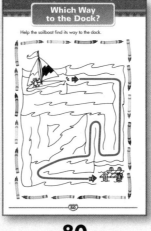

80

81